## THE G.I. SERIES

# U.S. Airborne Forces of the Cold War

**Front cover:** U.S. airborne troops on an operation in Vietnam. (U.S.N.A.)

Members of the 82nd Airborne Division carry out a practice jump in 1979. (U.S.N.A.)

THE G.I. SERIES

## THE ILLUSTRATED HISTORY OF THE AMERICAN SOLDIER, HIS UNIFORM AND HIS EQUIPMENT

# U.S. Airborne Forces of the Cold War

Leroy Thompson

Greenhill Books
LONDON

Stackpole Books
PENNSYLVANIA

Greenhill Books

*U.S. Airborne Forces of the Cold War* first published
2003 by Greenhill Books,
Lionel Leventhal Limited, Park House, 1 Russell
Gardens, London NW11 9NN
Email: info@greenhillbooks.com
Website: www.greenhillbooks.com
and
Stackpole Books, 5067 Ritter Road, Mechanicsburg,
PA 17055, USA

British Library Cataloguing in Publication Data:
U.S. Airborne forces of the Cold War. – (The G.I.
series: the illustrated history of the American soldier,
his uniform and his equipment; v.30)
1. United States. Army – Airborne troops. 2 Cold War
3. United States – Armed Forces – Airborne troops –
Uniforms 4. United States – Armed forces  - History –
20th century 5. United States – Armed forces –
Airborne troops – Equipment
I. Title
356.1'6'0973'09045

ISBN  1 85367 565 2

Library of Congress cataloging-in-publication data
available

Front cover illustration: U.S. airborne troops on an
operation in Vietnam

Edited by Donald Sommerville
Designed by David Gibbons, DAG Publications Ltd
Layout by Anthony A Evans, DAG Publications Ltd
Printed in China

# U.S. AIRBORNE FORCES
# OF THE COLD WAR

At the end of World War II, the United States found itself with five active airborne divisions. Over the first decade after the war's end various divisions were inactivated and in some cases reactivated. However, by the mid-1950s as the Cold War developed a more distinct chill, U.S. strategic doctrine seemed to indicate the need for two or three airborne divisions. The 82nd Airborne Division had become and would remain until today a key element of the U.S. strategic reserve. The XVIII Airborne Corps was reactivated in 1951 and has remained the controlling element for U.S. airborne forces until today.

Perhaps no airborne unit had quite the checkered post-war career of the 11th Airborne Division. After returning from occupation duties in Japan, the 11th had been deactivated but was reactivated in the early 1950s for occupation duty in Germany. When the 11th was deactivated once again in 1958, an airborne capability was retained in Europe with the activation of the 1st Brigade (Airborne) of the 24th Infantry Division, though this unit was shortly incorporated into the 8th Infantry Division. The 1st and 2nd Battalions of the 509th Parachute Infantry Regiment were the principal elements of the 1st Brigade (Airborne). Throughout the Cold War, the 509th PIR would remain the principal U.S. airborne unit assigned to Europe, though it was based in Italy (rather than Germany) during later

years. It was eventually redesignated as a battalion of the 325th Parachute Infantry, indicative of its links to the 82nd Airborne Division.

After World War II, the 101st Airborne Division was deactivated, though it was used as a paper entity for training airborne troops during the 1950s. Then, in 1956, the 101st was reactivated as a regular division. In 1957 the 101st was deployed to Little Rock, Arkansas, to enforce a federal order desegregating the schools there. The successor to the 11th Airborne Division in Europe, the 24th Airborne Brigade, also saw deployment in 1958 to Lebanon to help restore order to that country. Later, elements of the 82nd Airborne Division would replace the 24th in Lebanon. Potentially, the largest use of U.S. airborne forces since World War II occurred in 1963 during the Cuban Missile Crisis as the 82nd and 101st Airborne Divisions were 'chuted up awaiting orders to jump over Cuba.

During the early years of the Cold War, U.S. airborne divisions had retained virtually the same organization as during World War II, though glider infantry units had been phased out. In 1957-58, however, a major change took place when the airborne divisions were organized under the 'Pentomic' system which was intended to enhance combat effectiveness on the nuclear battlefield by dividing the parachute infantry units into five airborne battle groups. These battle groups were supported by airborne artillery batteries, as well as specialized airborne engineer, medical, signals, and other units.

In 1964 the airborne divisions were reorganized once again under what was known as the ROAD system. Under this organization, the airborne divisions had three brigades, each with three parachute infantry battalions and support troops. This organization allowed the divisions to be committed incrementally by brigades. As of 1964, the 82nd Airborne Division comprised the following units:

● 1st Brigade: 1/504th, 2/504th, 2/508th Parachute Infantry Battalions
● 2nd Brigade: 1/325th, 2/325th, 3/325th Parachute Infantry Battalions
● 3rd Brigade: 1/505th, 2/505th, and 1/508th Parachute Infantry Battalions
● Divisional Artillery: 1/319th, 1/320th, and 2/321st Airborne Artillery Battalions
● Division Support Command: HQ; HQ Company and Band; 782nd Maintenance Battalion; 307th Medical Battalion; 407th Supply and Transport Battalion; 82nd Administrative Company
● Separate Units: 82nd Aviation Battalion; 307th Engineer Battalion; 82nd Signal Battalion; 1/17th Cavalry; 82nd Military Intelligence Company; 82nd Military Police Company

The 82nd Airborne Division was assigned to the U.S. Strike Command in 1964 with the mission of acting as the United States' principal quick reaction unit. In 1965 this mission was affirmed when elements of the 82nd were deployed to the Dominican Republic to support the U.S.-backed military government in a civil war.

The tactical use of the helicopter as part of the "vertical envelopment" mission normally fulfilled by airborne forces became the role of the 11th Airborne Division when it was reactivated in 1963 as the 11th Air Assault Division. Intended to develop the tactics an airmobile force would use on the battlefield, the 11th Air Assault was soon needed in action when the U.S. commitment in Vietnam grew. Redesignated the 1st Cavalry Division (Airmobile), the division was deployed to Vietnam in September 1965, the first full U.S. Army division deployed. Initially, the 1st Brigade retained a full airborne capability, but this was discontinued in 1966. For the next five years, the Air Cav was sent wherever the fighting was heaviest, often turning the tide of battle. Although the 1st Cav was redeployed to the U.S.A. in April 1971, the 3rd Brigade remained in Vietnam until June 1972, when it was one of the last U.S. combat units to leave. After the Vietnam War, the 1st Cav was deactivated.

Another airborne unit, the 173rd Airborne Brigade, had been formed in June 1963, and trained for jungle warfare; though it was intended as the Pacific Command's quick reaction reserve, in May 1965, the 173rd deployed to Vietnam from Okinawa on temporary duty. The brigade would remain until August 1971 and see some of the heaviest fighting of the war. On February 22nd, 1967, as part of Operation Junction City, the 173rd carried out the only major combat parachute jump of the war, the first U.S. combat jump since the Korean War.

The 1st Brigade/101st Airborne Division followed the 173rd to Vietnam two months later in 1965. This separate airborne brigade fought for over two years on its own before the remainder of the 101st Airborne Division was deployed in November 1967. During the period 1968-69 the 101st Airborne was converted to an air assault division, though one brigade remained capable of airborne operations into the 1970s. After returning from Vietnam between December

1971 and March 1972 the 101st became America's only airmobile division.

Throughout the Vietnam War, the 82nd Airborne Division retained its role as the principal U.S. quick reaction unit. As part of this role, the 82nd kept (and still keeps) a Division Ready Force prepared for instant deployment anywhere in the world. However, as a result of the Tet Offensive, the 3rd Brigade, 82nd Airborne was deployed to Vietnam where it remained until December 1969. During this period the remaining two brigades of the 82nd remained the sole U.S. strategic reserve. As a result, a fourth brigade was temporarily formed to fill the gap left by the departure of the 3rd Brigade. When anti-Vietnam War sentiment and racial unrest resulted in civil disorder in some U.S. urban areas during 1967–68 elements of the 82nd Airborne were deployed to Detroit and Washington, DC.

Post-Vietnam, the 82nd and 101st Divisions remained the U.S. Army's key rapid deployment units but by the 1980s the 82nd Airborne Division was the U.S. Army's only true airborne division, the 101st having been converted to an Air Assault Division. The 82nd now had a strength of around 12,500 personnel organized under the regimental system as follows:

● 1st Brigade: 1/504th, 2/504th, 3/504th, and Company E (Anti-Armor) Parachute Infantry Battalions
● 2nd Brigade: 1/325th, 2/325th, 3/325th, and Company E (Anti-Armor) Parachute Infantry Battalions
● 3rd Brigade: 1/505th, 2/505th, and 3/505th, and Company E (Anti-Armor) Parachute Infantry Battalions
● Divisional Artillery: 1/319th, 2/319th, 3/319th Field Artillery Battalions; Battery B/26th Target Acquisition Battery
● Other Divisional Units: 1/17th Armored Cavalry Squadron; 3rd Battalion, 4th Air Defense Artillery; 4/68th Armor; 82nd Combat Aviation Battalion; 20th Aviation Battalion (AH-64 Attack Helicopters); 313th Military Intelligence Battalion; 307th Engineer Battalion; 82nd Signal Battalion; 82nd Military Police Company; Divisional HQ and HQ Company; 14th Chemical Detachment
● Divisional Support Command (DISCOM): 782nd Maintenance Battalion; 307th Medical Battalion; 407th Supply and Service Battalion; 82nd Administrative Company; 82nd Finance Company; 182nd Material and Management Center

The XVIII Airborne Corps under which the 82nd and 101st would serve during war time retained its own airborne military police, artillery, engineer, signals, aviation, and intelligence brigades.

Separate airborne units included the 36th Airborne Brigade of the Texas National Guard as well as some separate airborne battalions. The 1/509th at Vicenza, Italy, remained the principal U.S. airborne unit in Europe, though it was redesignated the 4/325th in 1983, and the 3/325th in 1986. The U.S. also normally maintained an airborne infantry unit in the Panama Canal Zone. Beginning in 1984, this was the 2/187th, but in 1987 it became the 1/509th. The 1/507th served as the airborne training battalion at Fort Benning, GA, from 1985. Airborne companies have been assigned to infantry units in Alaska, Korea, and elsewhere as well.

Although the 82nd Airborne Division was on alert at various times during the 1970s, as well as carrying out numerous overseas rapid deployment exercises and deploying battalions to the Sinai as part of the multinational observer force during 1981, the unit was not again committed to combat until 1983 when it took part in Operation Urgent Fury on Grenada. The parachute assault on Grenada was carried out by Army Rangers who seized an airfield which allowed the 1st and 2nd Brigades of the 82nd as well as divisional support units to be airlanded.

## Suggested Reading

Allen, Patrick H.F., *Screaming Eagles: In Action with the 101st Airborne Division (Air Assault)*; Mallard Press, New York, 1990.

Barker, Geoffrey, *A Concise History of the U.S. Airborne Army, Corps, Divisions, and Brigades*; Anglo-American Publishing Company, Brandon, FL, 1989.

Barker, Geoffrey, *A Concise History of the U.S. Army Airborne Infantry with Lineage and Insignia*; Anglo-American Publishing Company, Brandon, FL, 1989.

Berry, F. Clifton, Jr., *Sky Soldiers*, from "The Illustrated History of the Vietnam War"; Bantam Books, New York, 1987.

Halberstadt, Hans, *Airborne: Assault from the Sky*; Presidio Press, Novato, CA, 1988.

Mesko, Jim, *U.S. Infantry-Vietnam*; Squadron/Signal Publications, Carrollton, TX, 1983.

Mrazk, Steven, *The 82nd Airborne Division: "America's Guard of Honor"*; Taylor Publishing Company, Dallas, TX, 1987.

Rottman, Gordon, *U.S. Army Airborne, 1940-1990*, from "Osprey Elite Series"; Osprey, London, UK, 1990.

Stanton, Shelby, *Anatomy of a Division: 1st Cav in Vietnam*; Presidio Press, Novato, CA, 1987.

Stanton, Shelby, *U.S. Army Uniforms of the Vietnam War*; Stackpole, Harrisburg, PA, 1989.

Stanton, Shelby, *U.S. Army and Allied Ground Forces in Vietnam: Order of Battle*; U.S. News Books, Washington, DC, 1981.

Thompson, Leroy, *The All Americans: The 82nd Airborne*; David & Charles, Newton Abbot, UK, 1988.

Wildman, John Bennett, *1982, Year of the 82nd*; The Delmar Company, Charlotte, NC, 1982.

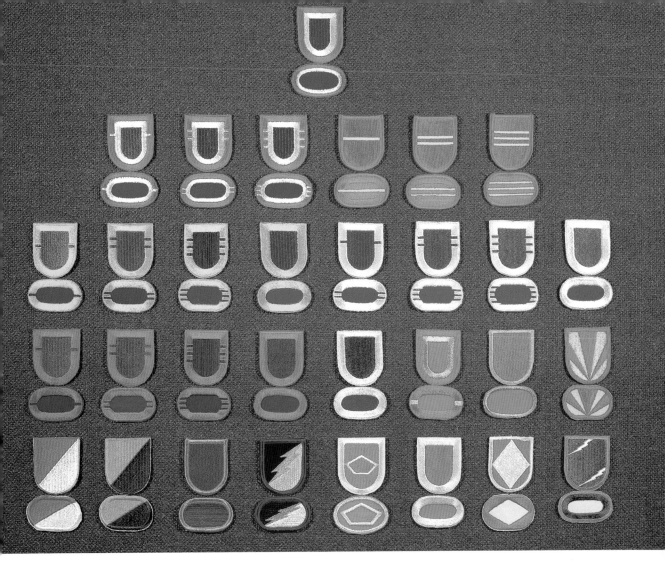

**Above:** Beret flashes and parachute ovals worn by units assigned to the 82nd Airborne Division. (Author's collection)

**Right:** Mortar crew of the 173rd Airborne Brigade fires an 81mm mortar in support of an operation north of Bien Hoa. (U.S.N.A.)

**Left:** An Army chaplain prepares for a jump during airborne training. Note the chaplain's cross on his helmet. (U.S.N.A.)

**Right:** Paratroopers of the 173rd Airborne Brigade pinned down by mortar fire during the assault on Hill 875 southwest of Dak To during November 1967. (U.S.N.A.)

**Right:** Members of the 173rd Airborne Brigade fire jeep-mounted 106mm recoilless rifles at suspected VC positions during a road security mission in February 1969. (U.S.N.A.)

**Opposite page, top:** 82nd Airborne troopers on deployment to Egypt. Note the desert camouflage and goggles necessary to protect against blowing sand. Troops being deployed to the desert have learned the value of goggles and high quality sun glasses. (U.S.N.A.)

**Opposite page, bottom:** An 82nd Airborne trooper prepares for a jump in Egypt. Note that the trooper on the right wears the maroon paratroop beret. (U.S. Army)

**Above:** Paratroopers undergoing basic airborne training at Fort Benning, GA, descend from the 250-foot tower. (U.S.N.A.)

**Left:** Members of the 82nd Airborne Division with a TOW anti-tank launcher. (U.S. Army)

**Below:** Members of the 82nd Airborne Division apply facial camouflage. (U.S. Army)

**Right:** A member of the 82nd Airborne Division with M16 rifle with M203 40mm grenade launcher attached. (U.S. Army)

**Bottom right:** 82nd Airborne 105mm howitzer battery in action. (U.S. Army)

82nd Airborne light machine-gunner in woodland camouflage training in the U.S.A. (U.S. Army)

**Above:** *Circa* the early 1960s, U.S. airborne troops board a C-123 prior to a practice jump. (U.S.N.A.)

**Below:** Early experiments with air mobility were carried out using helicopters such as this CH-34. (U.S.N.A.)

**Above:** 105mm howitzer, of the type used by U.S. airborne troops during the early post-war period, rigged for air drop in support of airborne operations. (U.S.N.A.)

**Opposite page:** Parachute rigger deflating a pilot 'chute with a closing tube during High-Altitude/Low-Opening (HALO) research during 1958 at Fort Bragg. (U.S.N.A.)

**Below:** Members of the 82nd Airborne Division take part in Exercise Swift Strike III during August 1963. (U.S.N.A.)

**Opposite page. top:** Members of the 82nd Airborne during the deployment of that unit to the Dominican Republic in 1965. (U.S.N.A.)

**Opposite page. bottom:** Elements of the 173rd Airborne Brigade are inserted by UH-1D helicopters on a search and destroy mission southeast of Saigon in August 1965. Note that the man in the left foreground carries a belt for the M60 General Purpose Machine Gun and the man to the right, probably a medic, carries a stretcher. (U.S.N.A.)

**Top:** Airborne and airmobile units often use the Chinook helicopter for heavy lift capability. (U.S.N.A.)

**Above:** Paratroopers of the 173rd Airborne Brigade carry out an air assault operation during 1965 near Phuoc Tuy. (U.S.N.A.)

**Above:** In Vietnam, members of the 1st Cav move towards a waiting UH-1D for an extraction. (U.S.N.A.)

**Opposite page, top:** Some members of the 101st Airborne Division carried tomahawks of this type for close combat during the Vietnam War. Others used more "conventional" close combat weapons such as sharpened entrenching tools. (Author's collection)

**Right:** In Vietnam, the helicopter proved a much more valuable tool for "vertical envelopment" than the parachute. (U.S.N.A.)

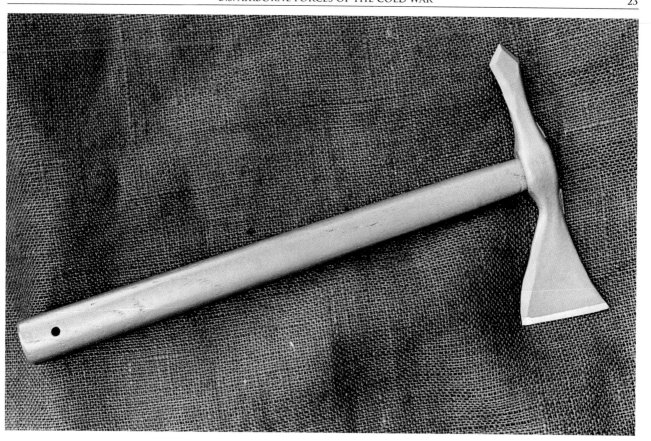

**Opposite page, top:** Members of the 173rd Airborne Brigade move out from Bien Hoa air base in May 1965. (U.S.N.A.)

**Opposite page, bottom:** Members of the 173rd Airborne Brigade take part in Operation Cedar Falls in the so-called Iron Triangle area of South Vietnam in January 1967. (U.S.N.A.)

**Above:** Members of the 173rd Airborne Brigade reach the top of a hill in the highlands of Dak To during Operation MacArthur in November 1967. They have set off a colored smoke grenade to identify their position for spotter planes. (U.S.N.A.)

**Left:** In the foreground, a captain in the 173rd Airborne Brigade orders his troops to move out after checking a hut for indications of Viet Cong presence during operations near Ben Cat in September 1965. Note that this early in the war, subdued insignia have not yet been issued and the captain wears visible rank insignia on the front of his helmet cover, thus making him a prime target for a VC sniper. Uniforms are the Army Tropical Uniform pattern. These "Sky Soldiers" also wear the M1956 Individual Load Bearing Gear. (U.S.N.A.)

**Lower left:** In August 1965, members of the 173rd Airborne Brigade move out on a search and destroy mission after a helicopter insertion. Note that they maintain good separation so that a mine or mortar round will be less likely to inflict multiple casualties. (U.S.N.A.)

**Right:** During October 1969, an 82nd Airborne sergeant prepares a barrel of phougas (a field expedient type of napalm) for use around the perimeter of an installation. (U.S.N.A.)

**Left:** The arrival of the 3rd Brigade, 82nd Airborne, in February 1968. This brigade was deployed to Vietnam in the wake of the Tet Offensive. The paratrooper in the foreground offers a good view of the Lightweight Rucksack frame. (U.S.N.A.)

**Right:** During May 1968, members of the 173rd Airborne Brigade carry out a search of the village of An Tac Tay #2.

**Below:** Members of the 1st Battalion, 508th Infantry, 82nd Airborne Division, during Operation Dirty Devil near Trung Lap during June 1969. Note that the two-color reversible camouflage helmet cover is worn. (U.S.N.A.)

**Left:** During December 1969, Brig Gen. George Dickerson, commander of the 3rd Brigade, 82nd Airborne Division, is presented with the Air Medal and Distinguished Flying Cross. Although Gen. Dickerson wears subdued insignia, his 82nd Airborne patch appears to be the full color version. (U.S.N.A.)

**Below left:** An 82nd Airborne Division captain briefs his troops during an operation near Trung Lap in June 1969. Note that the soldiers in left foreground and to the right of the captain wear issue tropical hats, though the one in the left foreground appears to be the camouflage model while the other appears to be OD (olive drab). Note that in addition to the 82nd Airborne patch on his left shoulder, the captain wears the "battle patch" of the 199th Light Infantry Brigade indicating a prior tour in Vietnam. (U.S.N.A.)

**Right:** Three locally made sniper patches for the primary airborne units deployed in Vietnam. (Author's collection)

**Opposite page, top:** Loading artillery aboard a U.S.A.F. transport aircraft for air transport. Although U.S. airborne units have the capability of dropping virtually all of their equipment, they rely heavily on air landing in actual fact. (U.S.N.A.)

**Left:** M56 Self-Propelled 90mm Anti-Tank Gun of the 101st Airborne Division. (U.S.N.A.)

**Above:** A Sheridan light tank of the type assigned to U.S. airborne units from the later 1960s. (U.S.N.A.)

**Left:** A weapon widely used by airborne and airmobile troops was the M79 40mm grenade launcher ("Thumper") which gave them an indirect fire capability. A good M79 grenadier could deliver rounds with great precision. Note that the grenadier in the right foreground carries "bug juice" in the rubber band around his helmet cover. (U.S.N.A.)

**Below:** In the foreground is a Light Weapons Carrier M274, the "Mechanical Mule" widely used by airborne troops. UH-1 Huey "Slicks" are landing in the background. (U.S.N.A.)

During an operation near Trung Lap in June 1969, a trooper of the 82nd Airborne Division uses an M2A17 portable flame thrower to destroy a hooch which had contained an enemy position. Note that he wears wet towels draped to help ward off the heat. (U.S.N.A.)

**Left:** An airborne trainee descending from the 250-foot tower at the parachute training school at Fort Benning, GA. (U.S.N.A.)

**Above:** An airborne trooper's equipment being checked prior to a jump. (U.S.N.A.)

**Right:** A paratrooper's view of the ground as his 'chute begins to open. (U.S.N.A.)

**Opposite page, top:** A CH-54 helicopter lifts a 155mm howitzer to a fire support base for the 173rd Airborne Brigade in Vietnam during September 1967.

**Opposite page, bottom:** Paratroopers of the 173rd Airborne Brigade in Vietnam. (U.S.N.A.)

**Above:** Paratroopers exiting during a jump; note the equipment bags for their rifles and other gear. (U.S.N.A.)

**Left:** An M551 Airborne Armored Fighting vehicle palletized for air delivery is pulled from a transport aircraft using the Low Altitude Parachute Extraction System (LAPES). (U.S.A.F.)

**Right:** During training in Egypt members of the 82nd Airborne Division rig for rappelling from a helicopter. (U.S.N.A.)

**Left:** Members of the 82nd Airborne Division with a jeep mounting an M60 machine gun. (U.S.N.A.)

**Above:** Mortar crewmen of the 82nd Airborne Division prepare to fire an 81mm mortar. (U.S.N.A.)

**Opposite page, top:** An airborne trainee exits the 34-foot jump tower at Fort Benning, GA. (U.S.N.A.)

**Opposite page, bottom: Above:** Airborne troops 'chuted up for a practice jump in Germany during 1966. These troops are from a special airborne "Long Range Patrol" unit assigned to the U.S. Seventh Army. (U.S.N.A.)

**Left:** An MP of the 82nd Airborne Division on patrol in the Dominican Republic. (U.S.N.A.)

**Right:** Member of the 82nd Airborne Division; note the use of the slits in the helmet cover for additional local flora camouflage. (U.S.N.A.)

**Left:** Member of the 82nd Airborne Division preparing to fire a LAW. (U.S.N.A.)

**Left:** Although they may be inserted onto the battlefield by parachute or helicopter, the airborne soldier is still an infantryman—as this member of the 82nd Airborne Division is well aware. (U.S.N.A.)

**Right:** 82nd Airborne Division personnel carry out a practice jump using the MC1-B-1 parachute during 1979. Note the equipment bags which have been lowered to hit the ground before the paratroopers. (U.S.N.A.)

**Below:** After a training jump in April 1981, troops of the 82nd Airborne Division turn in their parachutes. Note that they wear the woodland camouflage pattern. (U.S.N.A.)

**Left:** 82nd Airborne Division helicopter being loaded aboard a transport aircraft. (U.S. Army)

**Right:** A member of the 82nd Airborne Division with additional camouflage added to his helmet. Note the subdued 82nd Airborne SSI (shoulder sleeve insignia) along with the full color American flag. (U.S.N.A.)

**Left:** M551 Airborne Armored Fighting Vehicle being loaded aboard a C-130. (U.S.A.F.)

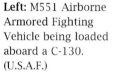

**Above:** 82nd Airborne Division
jeep-mounted TOW launcher.
(U.S. Army)

**Left:** 82nd Airborne troops
exiting a C-130 on a jump.
(U.S.A.F.)

**Right:** A member of the 82nd
Airborne Division prepares to fire
a Redeye anti-aircraft missile.
(U.S. Army)

**Opposite page, top:** A paratrooper of the 82nd Airborne Division gains control of his 'chute after a jump. He will collapse it, then fold it and place it into his kit bag. (U.S.N.A.)

**Opposite page, bottom:** Members of the 82nd Airborne Division after being dropped in Germany following a transatlantic flight in 1980 as part of Exercise Spearpoint '80. (U.S.N.A.)

**Above:** Members of the 82nd Airborne Division prepare a 107mm mortar for firing during live-fire training exercises in October 1981. (U.S.N.A.)

**Above:** Though designed to operate with less support than conventional infantry, airborne troops still need substantial logistical back-up. (U.S.N.A.)

**Below:** Enemy vehicles destroyed on Grenada by AC-130 gunships, supporting Rangers and elements of the 82nd Airborne Division. (Eagle)

M102 105mm Light Howitzer of the 82nd Airborne Division in action. (U.S. Army)

**Left:** A tanker of the 4/68th Armor of the 82nd Airborne Division loads .50 caliber rounds for the Browning M2 MG atop his M551. Note the woodland camouflage as well as the camouflaged tanker's helmet. Note also that tankers assigned to the 82nd Airborne Division are fully parachute qualified. (U.S.N.A.)

**Right:** Troops of the 82nd Airborne Division on an exercise in Germany. Note that the trooper in the foreground has a blank firing adaptor on his M16. (U.S.N.A.)

**Left:** Members of the 82nd Airborne prepare for a training jump in Egypt during a joint training exercise with Egyptian airborne troops. Note the jungle camouflage uniforms and subdued 82nd Airborne insignia. (U.S.N.A.)

**Above:** 82nd Airborne equipment can be rigged for parachute drop or parachute extraction as the transport aircraft flies near to the ground. (U.S.N.A.)

**Opposite page:** A member of the 82nd Airborne Division wearing a "Fritz" helmet and woodland camouflage carries an M16 with the M203 40mm grenade launcher attached. (U.S.N.A.)

**Below:** Airborne units' vehicles are designed for either air drop or air landing. (U.S.N.A.)

**Left:** The 82nd Airborne has female paratroopers who are fully airborne qualified. (U.S. Army)

**Above:** Members of the 82nd Airborne Division on deployment to Egypt prepare to assemble a tent. (U.S. Army)

**Right:** Two 82nd Airborne troopers preparing to move out after a training jump. (U.S.N.A.)

**Above:** Trooper of the 82nd Airborne Division on a training exercise in the early 1980s. Note that the M16 has the old-style Vietnam era triangular hand guard and the 20-round rather than 30-round magazine. However, the paratrooper wears the "Fritz" Kevlar helmet. Members of the 82nd Airborne were among the first troops to get this new helmet. (U.S.N.A.)

**Left:** Member of the 82nd Airborne Division on a training exercise. (U.S.N.A.)

**Right:** A member of the 82nd Airborne Division applies camouflage to his face during a training exercise. (U.S.N.A.)

**Left:** A member of the 82nd Airborne in full camouflage moves through the woods on a training exercise. (U.S.N.A.)

**Right:** An AH-64 Advanced Attack Helicopter of the type used by the 82nd Airborne Division and the 101st Air Assault Division. (U.S.N.A.)

**Right:** A member of the 82nd Airborne Division with the short version of the M60 GPMG used by airborne troops. (U.S. Army)

**Above:** A C-130 Hercules used to airland members of the 82nd Airborne Division during operations on Grenada. (Eagle)

**Left:** Enemy anti-aircraft gun captured by airborne forces on Grenada. (Eagle)

**Right:** An 82nd Airborne Division radioman. (U.S.N.A.)

**Left:** A member of the 82nd Airborne Division emplaces a claymore mine. (U.S.N.A.)

**Right:** 82nd Airborne gunners carrying out a fire mission against enemy positions on Grenada. (U.S.N.A.)

**Below:** 82nd Airborne Troops firing their 105mm howitzer against enemy positions on Grenada. (U.S.N.A.)

**Above:** 82nd Airborne troops on Grenada;. Note that the rear man is a grenadier with an M203 launcher mounted to his M16. He wears a special vest to carry the 40mm grenades. Note also that 30-round magazines are in place in the M16s. (Eagle)

**Below:** Helicopter gunships provide flying artillery for airborne and airmobile troops during training in Europe. (U.S. Army)

**Opposite page:** A member of the 82nd Airborne Division applies camouflage during an exercise. (U.S. Army)

Airborne troops descend in the sunset; though night drops are often the most effective in combat, they are also more difficult as troops tend to scatter more. (U.S.N.A.)